The Aftermath

Simon Rose

Weigl

Published by Weigl Educational Publishers Limited
6325 – 10 Street SE
Calgary, Alberta, Canada
T2H 2Z9

Website: www.weigl.ca

Library and Archives Canada Cataloguing in Publication

Rose, Simon, 1961-, author
        The aftermath / Simon Rose.

(Canada in World War I)
Includes index.
Issued in print and electronic formats.
ISBN 978-1-77071-249-2 (bound).--ISBN 978-1-77071-250-8 (pbk.).--
ISBN 978-1-77071-251-5 (epub)

        1. Canada--History--1918-1939--Juvenile literature. I. Title.

FC555.R68 2013   j971.061   C2013-904309-8
                                                    C2013-904310-1

Printed in the United States of America
1 2 3 4 5 6 7 8 9 0 17 16 15 14 13

072013
WEP130613

We acknowledge the financial support of the Government of Canada
through the Canada Book Fund for our publishing activities.

Photograph and Text Credits
Alamy: pages 6, 8, 11, 13, 26, 27, 28; Canadian Press Images: pages 11,
13; Getty Images: pages 1, 4, 5, 6, 8, 9, 10, 11, 12, 13, 14, 16, 18, 19, 20,
21, 22, 24, 25, 27; Glenbow Archives: page 11; iStockphoto: page 12;
McCord Museum: page 23

Every reasonable effort has been made to trace ownership and to obtain
permission to reprint copyright material. The publishers would be
pleased to have any errors or omissions brought to their attention so
that they may be corrected in subsequent printings.

Senior Editor
Aaron Carr

Art Director
Terry Paulhus

All of the Internet URLs given in
the book were valid at the time of
publication. However, due to the
dynamic nature of the Internet, some
addresses may have changed, or
sites may have ceased to exist since
publication. While the author and
publisher regret any inconvenience this
may cause readers, no responsibility for
any such changes can be accepted by
either the author or the publisher.

The Aftermath

CONTENTS

Many soldiers had lost good friends in the war.

Soldiers on both sides celebrated the war's end.

Some soldiers returned to their lives after suffering serious wounds in battle.

Newspapers became very important during the war.

The War Comes to an End

Canada's soldiers had served proudly, greatly influencing how Canada was viewed by the world.

After more than four years of fighting, World War I finally came to an end on November 11, 1918. Canada had played a major role in the war and had taken steps toward becoming an independent nation. Canadian forces were heavily involved in the final battles that secured victory for the **Allies**. Following the war, Canada signed the **Treaty of Versailles** independently of Great Britain and joined the **League of Nations**.

The war was over, but Canada had undergone a transformation between 1914 and 1918. The federal government had assumed a larger role in society during wartime, and some of the changes made during the war became permanent. Canadian society was also deeply divided. French Canadians had opposed **conscription** and were distrustful of the federal government. Canada's war effort had depended greatly on **labour unions**. When the war ended, these unions began to demand greater rights for workers and better working conditions. This led to unrest and work strikes, such as the Winnipeg **General Strike** in 1919.

The role of women had also changed during the war. With so many men fighting overseas, women entered the workforce in large numbers. They also won the right to vote in May 1918. When the war ended, tens of thousands of soldiers returned home to face an uncertain future with few available jobs. The Canadian government now faced the problem of adjusting from a wartime economy to a peacetime economy.

Making Peace

In March 1918, the Germans launched a final make-or-break **offensive** on the Western Front. Russia had withdrawn from the war the previous fall. After the Treaty of Brest Litovsk was signed between Russia and Germany, tens of thousands of experienced German troops were moved to the west. The Germans attacked on March 21, and the Allies were nearly overwhelmed. Fighting continued throughout the spring and early summer, but the Allies eventually recovered. They launched an offensive of their own in early August. Canadian soldiers were heavily involved in the final battles of the war, known as the Hundred Days Offensive. The war ended with an **armistice** at 11 a.m. on November 11, 1918.

Europe After the War

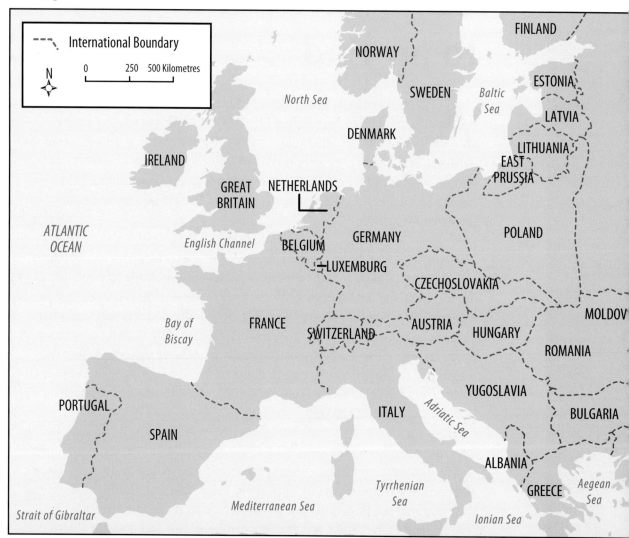

Peace negotiations took place the following year, culminating in the signing of the Treaty of Versailles on June 28, 1919. Though Canada was part of the British Empire, Prime Minister Robert Borden asked for Canada to have a separate seat at the peace conference. Borden pointed out that Canada had made a much larger contribution to the Allied victory than some of the smaller countries that were taking part in the negotiations. After some initial opposition, Canada was granted two seats at the conference. At different times, these seats were filled by Robert Borden, Sir George Foster, A. L. Sifton, and C. J. Doherty. When Canada signed the Treaty of Versailles independently of Great Britain, it helped move the young country toward full independence. It also greatly enhanced Canada's position on the world stage.

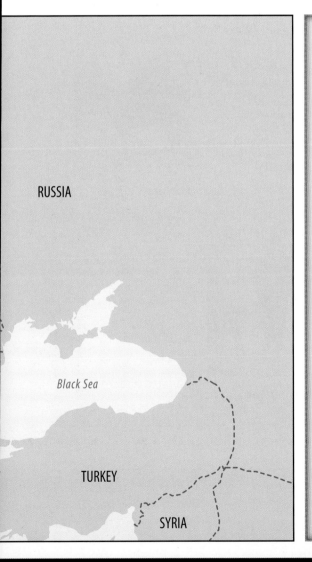

RUSSIA

Black Sea

TURKEY

SYRIA

Sir Robert Borden
(1854–1937)

Robert Borden was born in Grand Pre, Nova Scotia. After completing his education, Borden became a teacher, working at first in Nova Scotia then in the United States. When he returned to Canada, Borden became a lawyer. By 1890, he was the head of a respected law firm in Halifax, Nova Scotia.

In 1896, Borden was elected to the House of Commons. He became the leader of the Conservative Party in 1901. Borden spent the next 10 years rebuilding the party before winning the 1911 federal election. Borden served as prime minister during World War I and helped Canada play a larger role internationally. He served as prime minister until health problems led to his resignation in 1920. Borden died in Ottawa in 1937.

January - In Canada, Prime Minister Borden's conscription law, which had been passed in 1917, begins to be enforced.

March 3 - The Treaty of Brest Litovsk is signed by Germany and Russia.

March 21 - Germany launches an offensive on the Western Front.

May 24 - All female Canadian citizens aged 21 and over are given the right to vote in federal elections.

August 2 - Canada's first general strike takes place in Vancouver, British Columbia.

August 8 to November 11 - Canadian troops fight in several key battles during the Hundred Days Offensive.

September - The first cases of Spanish flu are reported in Canada. The influenza outbreak eventually kills about 50,000 people in Canada.

November 11 - World War I ends.

February 17 - Sir Wilfrid Laurier, leader of the Liberal party and former prime minister, dies.

April 17 - In New Brunswick, women are granted the right to vote.

May 15 to June 25 - The Winnipeg General Strike takes place.

May 20 - Women in Yukon win the right to vote.

June 6 - The government forms the Canadian National Railways from a number of unsuccessful private rail corporations.

June 28 - Canada signs the Treaty of Versailles.

September - The League of Indians of Canada holds its first meeting.

January 10 - Canada becomes a founding member of the League of Nations.

February 1 - The Royal Northwest Mounted Police and the **Dominion** Police are combined to create the Royal Canadian Mounted Police (RCMP).

February 26 - Canadian aboriginal peoples are granted the right to vote.

July 10 - Arthur Meighen replaces Robert Borden as prime minister.

October 17 - The first airplane to fly across Canada arrives in Richmond, B.C., from Halifax, N.S.

World War I changed the world, including Canada. There were a great number of economic and social shifts in countries around the world.

July 27 - Frederick Banting and Charles Best discover **insulin**.

November 21 - Canada is given a coat of arms, with the country's colours declared to be red and white.

December 6 - William Lyon Mackenzie King's Liberals win the federal election. Agnes Macphail becomes the first woman elected to the Canadian **Parliament**.

May 3 - Prince Edward Island grants women the right to vote.

September 18 - Mackenzie King refuses to support Great Britain in the Chanak Crisis, asserting Canadian independence in foreign affairs.

December - France grants Canada the land around Vimy Ridge to build a memorial to soldiers killed in World War I.

The Austro-Hungarian, Russian, Ottoman, and German Empires ceased to exist. After the war, other conflicts broke out on a smaller scale between individual countries. Canada's status continued to grow.

After the War

Canadians had made a large contribution to the Allies in World War I. After the war, the country had a more significant role in international politics and could assert more independence from Great Britain. Canada's economy had expanded during the war, new industries had been developed or expanded, and agricultural production had greatly increased. Many Canadians felt proud of these achievements and had a true sense of nationhood for the first time.

At home, Canadian society and the economy had undergone major changes. Women had entered the workforce and taken over jobs left by men serving overseas. This helped change the role of women in society in the following decades. Just before the war ended, women also won the right to vote in elections.

The effects of Canada's war effort were not all so positive. The war had created deep divisions in Canada, and there was a sense of unrest throughout the country. English and French Canadians were divided over the issue of conscription. Large numbers of people from various ethnic groups had been **interned** during the war, and they were resentful of the way they had been treated. Canadian workers also felt empowered by their contributions to the war effort. Their demands for better working conditions and more rights for workers would lead to labour unrest and many strikes in the years immediately after the war.

As soldiers began to return home, there were not enough jobs available to accommodate them. The government tried to help these soldiers re-enter society. The various measures implemented to help soldiers and their families formed the basis of Canada's healthcare and social welfare programs. When managing the war effort, the Canadian government had played a much larger role in the economy and in the lives of ordinary people. This included the recruitment of women into the workforce, the tight control of important industries, conscription of men into the armed forces, and the use of propaganda, or messages in the media that promote certain opinions and beliefs.

William Lyon Mackenzie King
Mackenzie King's stand against conscription earned him the support of Quebecers. This support helped King and the Liberals win the election of 1921.

Many women did not want to give up their jobs to returning soldiers.

Some soldiers were able to return to their old jobs.

Canada came out of the war as the world's leading exporter of wheat.

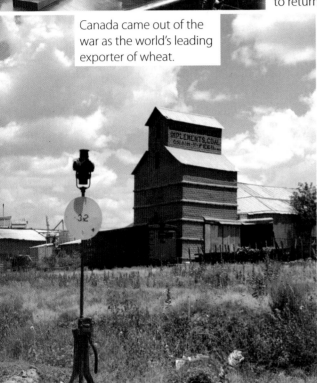

There were not enough jobs for the flood of returning soldiers.

Natural resource industries, such as logging, expanded greatly during the war.

Soldiers returning to their families tried to return to their normal lives.

Coming Home

Canadians who had served in the armed forces during World War I returned home to a country that was very different from the one they had left. The economy was in trouble, few jobs were available, and many soldiers struggled to adapt to civilian life. Some men returned home severely disabled, and many families had lost loved ones. The war created hundreds of thousands of veterans. This led to an expansion of both public and private support programs for Canadian soldiers and their families.

The Soldier Settlement Board

The Soldier Settlement Board was established in 1917 to help returning soldiers. The Board granted veterans up to 130 hectares of land to set up farms and provided loans for equipment, buildings, and livestock. Applicants for loans were investigated regarding their fitness, assets, skills, and suitability. Those without agricultural experience were often asked to work on a farm. The government provided pay for this type of training, and training centres were set up in some parts of Canada.

Pensions

The Canadian Board of Pension Commissioners was established in 1916 to determine pension rates for veterans. Compared to other countries, Canada treated its returning veterans very well. Soldiers received a cash payment when they left the armed forces, usually based on the length of their service. After World War I, Canada had the most generous military pensions in the world. Yet the sheer number of returning soldiers meant that veteran issues became one of the federal government's main responsibilities. In 1920, pensions for former soldiers accounted for more than 20 percent of federal expenditures.

Medical Treatment

In 1918, the Department of Soldiers' Civil Re-establishment was created to manage the return of large numbers of soldiers from overseas. The department assumed responsibility for the Military Hospitals Commission, which operated hospitals and homes for wounded soldiers. There were more than 30 hospitals, capable of caring for more than 6,500 patients. The social service branch cared for those soldiers with tuberculosis or with neurological or mental conditions, as well as those with injuries that affected their ability to work. The department also had a branch that worked with men who needed major dental treatment and those who had injuries to the jaw.

Soldiers with Disabilities

The Department of Soldiers' Civil Re-establishment paid disability allowances, with larger allowances for men with wives or families. Canada was the first Allied country to set up rehabilitation training for the disabled. Hospitals also began offering occupational therapy to help disabled veterans rejoin the workforce. Most men trained for work related to their former jobs, if they were still able to perform the tasks with their disability.

Soldiers blinded in the war or those with damaged vision received training at the Canadian National Institute for the Blind. In Toronto, the Department of Soldiers' Civil Re-establishment ran an artificial limb and surgical appliance factory. This factory mostly employed disabled former soldiers. There were fitting depots in other Canadian cities as well.

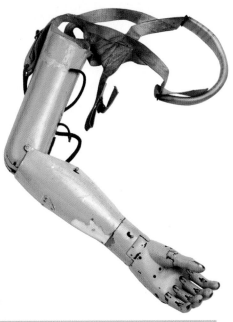

Employment

The Canadian and provincial governments established at least one employment office in every major city. The purpose of these offices was to provide vocational training and help former soldiers find jobs. The different governments shared information on job vacancies across the country. If men were willing to travel, special fares were arranged with the railway companies. This help stopped in 1920, when the poor economy led to large-scale unemployment. Disabled veterans continued to receive financial assistance, however.

The Post-war Economy

Canada was deeply in debt as a result of the huge cost of World War I. After rising throughout the war, Canada's economy began to decline in the years after the war. Companies that had been busy producing material for the war were closing down or reducing their workforce. The cost of living in Canada had risen by 64 percent since 1913. Companies and citizens alike found it difficult to keep up with **inflation** in the post-war years.

Some men got their former jobs back after the war, but many soldiers could not find work. Women now held jobs that had formerly been occupied by men. Many women did not want to return to what was considered a more traditional role at home. Most women remained part of the workforce, which reduced the number of jobs available to veterans of the war. Even with the assistance of government employment programs, jobs remained scarce.

Some people were opposed to the social welfare programs brought in by the government.

The Winnipeg General Strike

On May 1, 1919, Winnipeg's building and metal workers went on strike for higher wages. Two weeks later, the Winnipeg Trades and Labour Council appealed for a general strike. About 30,000 union and non-union workers walked out in support of the metal workers. Sympathy strikes also broke out in other parts of Canada. Winnipeg business leaders appealed for help from Ottawa. The **Russian Revolution** was a recent memory, and the federal government was afraid of similar events occurring in Canada. Federal employees were ordered to return to work or face dismissal. The mayor of Winnipeg replaced most of the city's police force with 1,800 special constables. Called Specials, these officers were issued horses and armed with baseball bats. The Royal North-West Mounted Police were also deployed to Winnipeg.

On June 10, the Specials tried to disperse a crowd of people listening to a speech. A riot broke out. A few days later, 12 union leaders were arrested, and the *Western Labour News* was banned from publication. The government also authorized the Mounted Police to use all necessary force to maintain order.

On June 21, war veterans organized a protest parade. A crowd of 6,000 people gathered at Winnipeg's city hall for the event. When a streetcar operated by strikebreakers approached, the veterans overturned the streetcar, which was set on fire. This caused the Specials and Mounted Police to charge at the crowd. On what became known as "Bloody Saturday," two strikers were killed, 34 were wounded, and 94 people were arrested. Worried about the possibility of more violence, workers decided to call off the strike. The strikers returned to work, and the largest social revolt in Canadian history was over.

> "Then with revolvers drawn, the Mounted Police galloped down Main Street, turned, and charged right into the crowd on William Avenue, firing as they charged. One man, standing on the sidewalk, thought the Mounties were firing blank cartridges until a spectator standing beside him dropped with a bullet through his breast .... Dismounted red coats lined up ... declaring military control."
>
> *Fred Dixon, editor of the* Western Labour News, *on the Winnipeg General Strike*

By the end of "Bloody Saturday," troops were in control of the streets. The strike was over, but it had shut down Winnipeg, Canada's third largest city at the time, for six weeks.

The Political Climate

Many farmers had enjoyed a boom time during the war because Great Britain had needed Canadian wheat and other crops.

New Political Parties

The decision of Prime Minister Borden's Conservative party to introduce conscription in 1917 had angered French Canadians. The Conservative Party found it difficult to win votes in Quebec for decades after the war. Voters in western Canada were also angry with the government. Farmers wanted to have free trade with the United States, but they were subjected to tariffs . This was a form of tax that meant farmers paid more for their equipment but made less profit from the sale of their products. Some farmers also felt that business leaders in Ontario and Quebec controlled the economy for their own benefit.

Ontario and prairie farmers formed the Progressive Party in 1920. In the 1921 federal election, the Progressive Party won 65 seats in Parliament. Although it was the second largest party in the House of Commons, the members of Progressive Party could not agree on policies. The economy improved in the 1920s as the Liberal Party introduced policies more favourable to farmers. This led to the decline of the Progressive Party. Some party members joined the Liberal or Conservative parties, while others later formed what later became the New Democratic Party.

Women in Politics

The 1921 election was the first in which women were allowed to vote. In this election, Agnes Macphail became the first woman ever elected to the House of Commons. This marked a shift in the 1920s as women started to become more involved in politics. Macphail campaigned for farmers, prison reform, pensions for seniors, and more rights for workers and women.

Nellie McClung had been a leading campaigner for women's voting rights before World War I. She had helped women to win the right to vote in Manitoba in 1916. McClung was one of the Famous Five, along with Emily Murphy, Henrietta Muir Edwards, Louise McKinney, and Irene Parlby. Together, they campaigned in 1927 to have women recognized as "persons" under the law, which helped women gain greater political rights in Canada.

Robert Borden retired as prime minister in 1920. He went on to have a successful business career.

In 1929, Agnes Macphail became the first Canadian woman to serve as a delegate to the League of Nations.

"When I first came to the House of Commons and walked out into the lobby, men sprang to their feet. I asked them to sit down since I'd come to walk around. I didn't want them doing me favours."

Agnes Macphail, first woman elected to the House of Commons in Canada

The Social Climate

Canadian society changed in many ways as a result of World War I. The government had intervened in society during the war years by creating income taxes, taking control of key industries, and regulating food and energy supplies. Programs had been put in place to help soldiers' families. Some of these programs later served as the foundation for Canada's welfare system.

When the factories that made shells and other weapons closed, many women moved into other kinds of factory work.

A number of programs and benefits were available to help returning veterans, but some former soldiers still found it very difficult to adjust to civilian life. Many Canadians lost family members during the war, in many cases losing their main wage earner. This placed many families in difficult circumstances. Charitable organizations were able to provide some help, but the hardships suffered by many families severely stretched the country's resources. Some families also had to make major adjustments, as they learned how to look after disabled relatives who had been severely wounded in the war.

The role of women in society had also changed, and women no longer saw themselves as simply homemakers and childcare providers. Many of the women who remained in the workforce after 1918 were determined to have careers of their own. Canadians also faced a severe threat just as the war ended. Even soldiers who had survived the horrors of the trenches could be struck down by the Spanish flu.

"At a meeting of the Charlottetown Board of Health... (it was) decided by a resolution unanimously that, in view of the prevalence of influenza in the city and in order to prevent its further spread, the churches, schools, and theatres be closed until further notice."

The Guardian, *October 7, 1918*

The Spanish Flu

The Spanish flu was a global **pandemic** that killed more than 20 million people around the world between 1918 and 1919. The first cases of flu were reported in the spring of 1918, and the disease spread rapidly in Europe. Spain was not involved in World War I, so the press there was not censored and was free to report on the spread of the flu. This led people to believe that the disease had started in Spain. It seemed to have died out by July, but a second, highly contagious strain of the flu virus appeared in the fall that proved deadly.

It is believed more than 260,000 people died of Spanish influenza in Spain.

Spanish flu arrived in Canada in September 1918. Many soldiers returning home from the war in Europe carried the disease back to Canada with them. The disease killed old and young alike, but it was particularly dangerous to people between 20 and 35 years of age. At least a quarter of Canadians were infected by the flu. There were very few families that did not lose at least one family member to the disease. The flu spread quickly, and its victims could be dead within a day or two. Some died only hours after showing the first signs of illness. Even those who survived the infection were so weakened that they often caught and died from other infections, such as pneumonia.

By the time the outbreak died down, it had killed about 50,000 Canadians. In response to this event, the federal government created the Department of Health in 1919 to co-ordinate all of the country's health programs.

Rebuilding the Country

The Canadian economy struggled after the war, and unemployment was high. The country also struggled to pay off the debts it had taken on during the war. Times were hard for Canadians for the first few years after the war, but by the mid-1920s, the economic situation began to improve.

Canadian National Railways, later known as CN Rail, was created in 1919. The federal government formed the company from a number of unsuccessful private rail companies. CN Rail inherited a huge debt from these companies but eventually became a successful business.

Foreign investors slowly regained confidence in Canada, and the country slowly began to develop new industries again. There was also an increased foreign demand for Canada's natural resources. European countries that were still suffering from the aftermath of the war needed food. Canadian farmers began to produce larger crops, which led to more profits. Many farmers invested in trucks, tractors, and other farming machinery. Across the prairies, production increased. The price of wheat rose, and the grain elevators were well stocked.

CN Rail played a large role in the rebuilding of the Canadian economy after the war.

Demand from the American pulp and paper industry resulted in a large increase in pulp exports to the United States. This created many much-needed jobs in Canada. New Canadian industries and the growth of towns and cities increased the demand for electricity. Canada's extensive river systems soon made the county the world's second largest producer of hydroelectric power. American financing helped to develop new metal and mineral deposits, which provided Canadians with both wealth and jobs. More factories and the growth of the automobile industry increased demand for oil and gas. Oil had been discovered in Alberta in 1914, and this led to the development of the petroleum industry and an increase in population in western Canada in the following decades. Canada's economy continued to improve until 1929, when the Great Depression began.

Lumber companies all around Canada benefited from the American need for pulp.

"The War is over, and for a long time to come it is going to take all that the energies of man can do to bridge the chasm and heal the wounds which the War has made in our social life."

William Lyon Mackenzie King, May 1919

Leading Canadians

William Lyon Mackenzie King (1874–1950)

Mackenzie King was leader of the Liberal party from 1919 to 1948 and served as prime minister for almost 22 years.

King was born in Berlin, Ontario, which later became Kitchener. King was elected to Parliament in 1908 and became minister of labour.

King became leader of the Liberal party in 1919 and won the 1921 election to become prime minister. He strongly asserted Canada's independent position in 1922 over the Chanak Crisis, when Great Britain almost went to war with Turkey and expected Canadian support. King insisted the decision had to be made by the Canadian Parliament, not by Great Britain. He lost the 1925 election but soon retuned as prime minister before losing again in 1930. He was elected again in 1935 and served as prime minister until 1948.

Arthur Meighen (1874–1960)

Arthur Meighen was the leader of the Conservative party and served as prime minister of Canada from 1920 to 1921 and briefly again in 1926.

Meighen was elected to the House of Commons in 1908. He worked on the creation of Canadian National Railways and was involved in the decision to use force in the 1919 Winnipeg General Strike.

Meighen became prime minister in 1920, but his stance on issues such as conscription and farming made him unpopular with many voters. Meighen's Conservatives lost the next election. Meighen even lost his own seat in Parliament. Mackenzie King became prime minister, and Meighen became leader of the Opposition. He became prime minister again in 1926, but only held the position for three months. He retired from politics in 1942.

Frederick Banting (1891–1941)

Frederick Banting was a medical scientist and doctor awarded the **Nobel Prize** in Medicine in 1923. He was the main discoverer of insulin, which is used to help people suffering from diabetes.

Banting graduated from the University of Toronto in 1916 and enlisted in the Canadian Army Medical Corps. In 1918, he was wounded at the Battle of Cambrai but continued helping other wounded men. He was awarded the Military Cross for bravery in 1919.

After the war, Banting took an interest in diabetes. Working with Dr. Charles Best, the two men saved a boy's life in 1922 with the first ever dose of insulin. Banting and his colleague J. J. R. Macleod were awarded the Nobel Prize jointly in 1923. The Canadian government granted Banting a lifetime **annuity** to continue his research.

Agnes Campbell Macphail (1890–1954)

Agnes Campbell Macphail was the first woman to sit in the Canadian Parliament. She was the only woman elected to the House of Commons in 1921, when women were first allowed to vote in federal elections.

Macphail was born in Grey County, Ontario. She joined the United Farmers of Ontario and was elected to Parliament in 1921. She was later re-elected three times.

Macphail supported farming issues, but also championed workers' rights, pensions for seniors, and women's rights. In 1939, Macphail founded the Elizabeth Fry Society of Canada, which supported prison reform. She was active in the Women's International League for Peace and Freedom. At the League of Nations, Macphail worked on the World Disarmament Committee. She died in Toronto in 1954.

Frederick Ogilvie Loft (1861–1934)

Also known by his Mohawk name Onondeyoh, Frederick Ogilvie Loft was an Aboriginal activist who founded the League of Indians of Canada.

Loft was born on the Six Nations Reserve near Brantford, Ontario. He grew up speaking both English and Mohawk. Loft worked many jobs before taking an interest in native affairs in the early years of the 20th century.

When World War I began, Loft visited Ontario reserves to promote enlistment. He was sent overseas in 1917. While serving in Europe, the Six Nations Council gave Loft a pine tree chieftainship. This was an honour given to the most outstanding members of the Iroquois Confederacy. In 1919, Loft created the League of Indians of Canada. His goal was to create an organization like the League of Nations for Canada's First Nations.

Sir George Eulas Foster (1847–1931)

Sir George Eulas Foster served as a **cabinet minister** for seven Canadian prime ministers. He was a member of the House of Commons or senator for more than 45 years and was one of Canada's representatives at the Paris Peace Conference in 1919.

Foster was born in Carleton County, New Brunswick. He graduated from the University of New Brunswick and worked there for several years. Foster was elected to the House of Commons in 1882 and served in Conservative governments until 1896.

When Robert Borden won the election in 1911, Foster became minister of trade and commerce. He was briefly Canada's prime minister when Borden became ill in 1920. Foster was appointed to the Senate in 1921. He died in 1931 in Ottawa.

Canada's Peace

Canadians served in many different areas during World War I. Most of the fighting they were involved in took place in a small area of northern France and Belgium, but soldiers, airmen, sailors and nurses also served in the eastern Mediterranean, on ships in the Atlantic Ocean, and at ports and training facilities across Canada. Soldiers from Newfoundland were involved in the Gallipoli campaign in Turkey. Canadian nurses tended to the wounded from the Salonika front in northern Greece and from the fighting in Gallipoli. Nurses were also among those killed when the hospital ship *Llandovery Castle* was sunk by a German U-boat in June 1918 off the southern coast of Ireland.

The sinking of the hospital ship *Llandovery Castle* was considered illegal under international agreements. After the war, the U-boat captain who ordered its sinking was charged with war crimes.

By the Numbers

Canada had changed in many ways during World War I, and it continued to change in the years after the war as well. Changes in Canada's economy led to a migration of workers away from rural areas, especially on the east coast. Populations in cities rose, and Canada increased its raw material exports.

Canada's Mineral Production, 1927

90% of world nickel

55% of world cobalt

9.0% of world gold

8.7% of world lead

8.4% of world silver

6.4% of world zinc

4% of world copper

Population Distribution in Canada's Provinces and Territories, Before and After the War (by percentage)

PROVINCE/ TERRITORY	1911		1921	
	Rural	Urban	Rural	Urban
Prince Edward Island	84.03	15.97	78.45	21.55
Nova Scotia	62.20	37.80	56.66	43.34
New Brunswick	71.71	28.29	67.92	32.08
Quebec	51.80	48.20	43.99	56.01
Ontario	47.43	52.57	41.83	58.17
Manitoba	56.57	43.43	57.12	42.88
Saskatchewan	73.32	26.68	71.10	28.90
Alberta	63.22	36.78	62.12	37.88
British Columbia	48.10	51.90	52.81	47.19
Yukon	54.59	45.41	68.58	31.42
Northwest Territories	100	-	100	-

Home Front Statistics

$2 BILLION debt Canada incurred during war

$737 average yearly wage in Ottawa in **1911**
$1,351 average yearly wage in Ottawa in **1921**

1919 the end of Prohibition, or the ban on alcohol, in Quebec

138,800 immigrants to Canada in **1920**
165,000 immigrants to Canada in **1929**

1920 the first time Canada's Group of Seven artists show their work together

17% percentage of all women over 15 years of age working in **1920**

65% percentage of all women in the workforce working in domestic, clerical, or professional occupations by **1921**

112 seats won by Mackenzie King's Liberals in the **1921** election

5 the number of Hollywood movies made in Canada between 1922 and 1923

1923 the first year Canada sells more products to the United States than to Great Britain

17% unemployment rate in **1923**

2.5 MILLION number of workers on strike in B.C. in **1926**

47,427 British immigrants in **1926**
9,674 German immigrants in **1926**

1929 the first year women could sit in the Canadian senate

31 age of Agnes Macphail when she became a member of Parliament

War and Remembrance

Canada mobilized more than 620,000 soldiers for World War I. More than 60,000 Canadians were dead or missing as a result of the war, with about 150,000 wounded. The war affected everyone in the country. People wanted to honour those who had served in the war.

Remembrance Day

In 1931, the Canadian government passed the Armistice Remembrance Day Act. This fixed the date for Remembrance Day as November 11. This was originally to commemorate the sacrifice of Canadians in World War I and a number of earlier conflicts. The date now honours all those who served in World War I, World War II, the Korean War, and all conflicts since in which Canadian forces have served. Each year on November 11, special ceremonies are held in towns and cities across Canada to remember those who served their country in time of war.

Many of the ceremonies take place at war memorials or at special monuments called **cenotaphs**. Prayers and commemorative poems are usually read aloud at these ceremonies. There are also often parades by both veterans and those currently serving in the armed forces. After the parades, a bugler plays "The Last Post," a tune symbolizing saying farewell to those who have died. After two minutes of silence, the bugler plays another tune called "Reveille." This one serves as a reminder that the memory of those who have died will always live on in people's hearts and minds.

War Memorials

Many towns and cities in Canada have cenotaphs and war memorials, honouring those members of the local community who died in war. The National War Memorial on Parliament Hill in Ottawa depicts uniformed figures passing through an archway, representing those Canadians who volunteer to serve in the armed forces. On Remembrance Day, thousands of people gather at the National War Memorial and other monuments to pay tribute to those Canadians who serve their country. The Tomb of the Unknown Soldier, also in Ottawa, was built in 2000.

The National War Memorial in Ottawa was unveiled in 1939.

The dedication on the Vimy Memorial reads "To the valour of their countrymen in the Great War and in memory of their sixty thousand dead, this monument is raised by the people of Canada."

The red poppy was chosen as a symbol of remembrance because of the poppies that grew on the graves of fallen soldiers in Belgium.

It is a tradition to lay wreaths at the National War Memorial on Remembrance Day.

The Tomb of the Unknown Soldier contains the remains of a Canadian soldier who died at the battle of Vimy Ridge.

The Seeds of War

World War I was called the "War to End All Wars." Yet, within 21 years of World War I ending, global conflict again broke out. It has been said that World War I actually caused World War II. How could this be?

Using the Internet, books from the library, and any other resources, determine what aspects of World War I contributed to the next world war.

Be sure to examine the following areas:

- The conditions of the Versailles Treaty and the political and economic problems it may have created.
- The state of the global economy following World War I.
- Societal changes created by World War I that may have led to more conflict.

Draw a concept web based on your findings, and use the concept web to help you write a report on your findings.

Concept Web

- Could World War II have been avoided?
- What could have been done at the end of World War I to prevent another global war from occurring?

- What did you learn from your research?
- Would you suggest these books or websites to others?
- Was anything missing from these sources?

- What were the main causes of World War II that can be traced back to World War I?
- What else contributed to World War II?

YOUR OPINION

LESSONS

CAUSES

Seeds of War

OUTCOME

EXPLOSION

EFFECTS

- What was the outcome of World War II?
- Did the countries involved learn any lessons from World War I?
- Was the resolution of World War II better than the treaties that ended World War I?

- What was the first act of World War II?
- What was the response to this act?
- Could the war have been stopped at this point or was it too late?

- How exactly did these causes bring about World War II?
- Did anyone raise concerns about these issues and offer solutions?
- Was anything done to try to stop World War II before it started?

Test Your Knowledge

1 Which Canadian prime minister led Canada in the years after World War I?

2 Which four Canadians represented Canada at the Paris Peace Conference?

3 Who was the first woman elected to the Canadian House of Commons?

4 When was Bloody Saturday?

5 Who founded the League of Indians of Canada?

6 How many Canadians are believed to have died from the Spanish flu?

7 For what invention did Frederick Banting the Nobel Prize?

8 How many seats in Parliament did the Progressive Party win in the 1921 election?

9 Who replaced Robert Borden as prime minister in 1920?

10 Which department helped former soldiers set up farms and apply for loans?

Further Resources

CHECK IT OUT!

www.warmuseum.ca/cwm/
exhibitions/guerre/home-e.aspx

www.canadaatwar.ca/page43.html

www.thecanadianencyclopedia.
com/articles/first-world-war-wwi

http://canadasnavalmemorial.ca/
history/battles-and-conicts/world-
war-i-1914-1918

Glossary

Allies: relating to the forces of Great Britain, France, and Russia, including all related territories and colonies; later including Italy (1915) and the United States (1917)

annuity: a sum of money payable yearly or at other regular intervals

armistice: agreement to stop a war

cabinet minister: a high-ranking member of a government

cenotaphs: monuments honouring victims of war

conscription: compulsory enrolment in the armed forces

dominion: a self-governing territory of an empire

general strike: a mass work stoppage involving all trades or industries

inflation: a general increase in prices and a fall in the purchasing value of money

insulin: a protein produced by the pancreas that is necessary for the human body's normal use of glucose

interned: forcibly confined to an internment camp

labour unions: organized associations of workers formed to protect workers' rights

League of Nations: an international organization founded at the end of World War I to preserve peace around the world

Nobel Prize: an annual prize awarded to those who have made great achievements for the benefit of humanity

offensive: an attack launched by military forces against the enemy

pandemic: a disease affecting people over a wide geographic area

Parliament: the highest law-making body of the Canadian government

Russian Revolution: the 1917 overthrow of the Russian monarchy that resulted in the creation of a new government

Treaty of Versailles: the 1919 agreement between the Allies and Germany that forced Germany to give up many of its territories and accept full responsibility for the war

Index